THE CAREER RESOURCE LIBRARY

Careers
in
MAGAZINE PUBLISHING

Toni L. Rocha

The Rosen Publishing Group, Inc.
NEW YORK

This book is dedicated to my mother, Lois M. Jarley, a female pioneer in advertising. She opened her own agency in the late 1950s and operated it successfully for nearly thirty years. I learned more from her than I can ever begin to express.

Published in 2001 by The Rosen Publishing Group, Inc.
29 East 21st Street, New York, NY 10010

Copyright © 2001 by Toni L. Rocha

First Edition

Library of Congress Cataloging-in-Publication Data

Rocha, Toni L.
　　Careers in magazine publishing / by Toni L. Rocha.—1st ed.
　　　　p. cm.—(Career resource library)
　　Includes bibliographical references and index.
　　ISBN 0-8239-3188-9
　　　　1. Periodicals—Publishing—Vocational guidance.
I. Title. II. Careers (Rosen Publishing Group).
Z286.P4 R63 2000
070.5'72'023–dc21
　　　　　　　　　　　　　　　　　　　　00-010830

Manufactured in the United States of America

About the Author

Toni L. Rocha retired in December 1999 from her position as police and fire reporter for the *Beloit Daily News* in Beloit, Wisconsin. She has more than thirty years' experience writing in various areas of the communications field, including advertising. Currently, she writes from her home in Roscoe, Illinois. Ms. Rocha travels, works counted cross-stitch, takes nature photographs, renders pen-and-ink drawings, carves wood, creates miniatures, gardens, and reads—a lot.

Acknowledgments

This book could not have been written without the generous contributions in time, effort, and advice of those whose names you will find within its chapters. My thanks goes beyond those visible supporters to wonderful people such as: Jennifer McCoy in Public Relations at Meredith Corporation. She took the time to email several colleagues asking if they would agree to interviews and networked us all together. Ted Kreiter, managing editor at the *Saturday Evening Post*, introduced me, electronically, to Holly Miller a fantastic writer and editor. Many more directed me to the most appropriate sources without hesitation. And finally, thanks to my editor, Maia Miller, who awaited each installment with endless patience.

Contents

Introduction

Today you see magazines everywhere you go: at home, in libraries and bookstores, pharmacies and supermarkets, barber shops and beauty salons, at school, and in doctors' offices. These colorful publications are so familiar, you may not give them a second thought. You have, no doubt, read magazines for enjoyment and used articles from magazines for classes at school.

Who creates these magazines, and how? Certainly, popular newsstand magazines such as *Vogue, Seventeen,* and *Newsweek* rely on a large staff of editors, designers, and photographers to produce each issue. But the publishers of smaller magazines, such as literary journals, also depend on trained, knowledgeable, and creative people to put together a successful product.

Every magazine, whether it is sold at newsstands or through the mail, represents the work of publishers, editors, writers, artists and photographers, graphics technicians, distributors, and sales personnel. With an estimated 60,000 magazines published weekly and monthly in the

German craftsmen invented movable type during the fifteenth century.

United States alone, and an average of 300 new titles launched each year, a vast array of career opportunities awaits you in magazine publishing.

The History of the Magazine

Magazine publishing began nearly four centuries ago. According to *Merriam Webster's Encyclopedia of Literature*, today's magazines evolved from printed pamphlets, broadsides, and chapbooks, in the early 1500s. Not long after German craftsmen invented movable type in the 1450s, small print shops appeared across Europe and flourished in response to the increased demand for news and accessible reading material.

Pamphlets

Pamphlets were among the first publications. Simple and unbound, these pamphlets often contained religious or political propaganda and were widely distributed in

England, France, and Germany. The text ranged from cleverly abusive to downright nasty. Because pamphlets spread gossip, scandal, rumor, and intrigue involving people in high government and religious positions, they were immensely popular and influential.

Today, pamphlets (or brochures) serve a variety of purposes. Businesses frequently use them to advertise their products. Nonprofit organizations design pamphlets to outline the services they offer their clients, solicit donations, or inform the public about a broad range of subjects. You have probably read a few from the YMCA, your church, or your school.

Broadsides

Broadsides were large sheets of paper with text printed on one side. These were hawked on the streets in the same way that newsboys used to sell newspapers on city street corners. The text, called a broadside ballad, was commonly written in verse form and described recent crimes, executions, and disasters. Sometimes the news was read aloud or sung for those who could not read. Troubadours, whose voices carried the news throughout the land, often set these verses to music. The printing of lyrics to traditional ballads on broadsides helped preserve songs that might otherwise have been lost to us today.

Chapbooks

Chapbooks were small, inexpensive, stitched books or pamphlets peddled across Europe and America by itinerant dealers called chapmen. Illustrated with woodcuts, chapbooks focused on popular heroes, legends, folklore, jokes, famous crimes, nursery rhymes, school lessons, Biblical tales, dream lore, and more. Printed in multiples of four pages, chapbooks most closely resembled today's magazines. As time passed, some of these publications began to be issued at regular intervals, which may explain why magazines are sometimes referred to as "periodicals."

Early Magazines

One of the first true magazines was *Erbauliche Monaths-Unterredungen*, or *Edifying Monthly Discussions*. It was published in Germany from 1663 to 1668. Read by the intellectuals of Europe, this publication is comparable to modern magazines such as *Psychology Today* and the *Journal of the American Medical Association*.

By the early 1800s, ambitious publishers identified a bigger market. Magazines evolved for a less educated audience and featured articles on fashion, religion, entertainment, and family life. Illustrated with woodcuts and engravings, they were published on weekly, monthly, and quarterly schedules.

In the United States, one of the most popular and successful of these was *Godey's Lady's Book*, published from 1830 to 1898. American women viewed it as a source of fashion news and a guide to social etiquette. *Godey's Lady's Book* also featured articles written by influential artists and intellectuals, such as Ralph Waldo Emerson, Henry Wadsworth Longfellow, Edgar Allan Poe, Nathaniel Hawthorne, and Harriet Beecher Stowe.

In the late 1800s and early 1900s, publishers benefited from many technological advances, including the inventions of the rotary press and the halftone process that enabled publishers to incorporate photographs into their magazines. Also, the increasing availability of inexpensive paper and the creation of magazine advertising began to offset the cost of printing and publishing not covered by subscription fees. These changes combined to make magazine publishing a profitable business. As the industry grew, so too did the number and diversity of career opportunities.

From these simple beginnings more than 400 years ago, magazine publishing has grown to become a $10 billion-a-year industry. In the following chapters, you will learn more about different types of magazines and the career possibilities they offer. You will also see what it takes to be a part of this vast, expanding, and ever evolving field.

More than 300 new magazines are launched each year.

Defining the Field

1

A woman thumbs through *Vogue* while waiting at the dentist's office. A student scans *Newsweek* and *Time* as part of a social studies assignment. An electrical engineer, at her drawing board, reads a trade magazine devoted to breakthroughs in her field. A busy father takes a time-out with a cup of coffee and peruses the latest issue of *Child*.

Each day, millions of Americans turn to magazines for information, news, and entertainment. As they do this, they rely on a workforce estimated at more than 100,000 to consistently produce magazines filled with important insights and useful information. If you were to flip through the pages of *Seventeen*, you would find dozens of color photographs accompanying news articles and short stories written primarily by freelance authors. You might read regular columns and features that run each month. You would also see pages and pages of advertising. These ads serve two purposes: to inform you about new consumer products and to help underwrite the cost of producing the magazine.

As you can imagine, it takes a large staff to produce *Seventeen,* whose circulation has grown to more than 2.5 million. Magazines such as *Seventeen* thrive because the staff is constantly aware of the changing viewpoints and needs of readers. At the same time, *Seventeen's* editors hold fast to the high standards of content and quality its readership expects. The same is true of all successful magazines worldwide, regardless of their focus.

What Is a Magazine?

Magazines come in all shapes and sizes, from the compact *Reader's Digest* to oversized magazines such as the former monthly *Life.* Some publications look like magazines but call themselves newspapers, while others that look like newspapers call themselves magazines. Professionals inside the industry often refer to magazines as "titles" or "books." Yet many readers think of a magazine as a periodical because it is published on a regular basis: daily, weekly, monthly, quarterly, or semi-annually. Some smaller or literary magazines are published just once each year.

Nevertheless, there are elements common to all magazines. While newspapers publish factual articles about a variety of current events, magazines have a more narrow focus, appealing to the specific interests of their readers. Also, magazines may include both fiction and nonfiction articles. Generally though, magazines fall into two broad categories: consumer and trade.

Consumer Magazines

Consumer magazines outnumber trade magazines. Consumer magazines focus on just about anything that interests people. Food, travel, pets, crafts, music, fashion, collectibles, antiques, sports, gardening, decorating, art, computers, parenting, health—the topics are nearly endless. Additionally, for people who simply enjoy reading, general interest magazines and newsweeklies are a compelling diversion.

Trade Magazines

Trade magazines, on the other hand, are published for professionals in the global business community. These magazines such as *Fleet Owner* or *Restaurant Show Daily* frequently center on particular industries. Or, they cater to people in specific occupations, like *Video Engineering* or *Data Communications*. Focused primarily on reporting cutting-edge industry trends and state-of-the-art technological advances, these publications are intensely researched and narrow in scope.

Most trade and consumer magazines have Web sites on the Internet as well. A few magazines, *Omni* for example, have switched from printing hard copy issues to publishing solely on the Web. In fact, a growing number of magazines often referred to as "e-zines" publish exclusively on the Internet.

Magazines can be entirely staff-written and designed in-house. But the majority rely on the highly competitive freelance writing, illustrating, and photography market for obvious reasons. It is more cost-effective than hiring a writer or photographer full-time. Also, the editors can take advantage of the thriving freelance market to cultivate young professionals who bring fresh insight and different perspectives to each issue.

But all magazines, regardless of size, circulation, and focus, require at least a minimum number of staff

It takes teamwork to put together a magazine.

members. From the individual desktop publisher to the newsweekly *Time* that relies on 300 full-time editorial staff members, this is a field with great career potential!

Who's Who?

Within the first few pages of any magazine, you will find what is referred to in the publishing industry as a masthead. This boxed list includes the names and titles of all staff members in management positions, as well as the magazine's address, the telephone numbers for each department, and the Web address.

For example, the masthead for *Midwest Living* identifies the editor-in-chief, an executive editor, an art director and two associates, a senior writer, a contributing writer, and several administrative assistants. Its staff includes editors for food, home, garden, copy and production, special assignments, photography, special publications, and a contributing editor for travel.

Beneath these credits, *Midwest Living* also lists the advertising staff, marketing and circulation directors, a research director and manager, a director of operations, and a direct response director, plus promotional and associate marketing managers. In addition to those positions listed on the masthead, there are many other people working in each division. All totaled, *Midwest Living*'s masthead mentions sixty-five people.

The size of a magazine staff can vary greatly, depending on a magazine's budget, circulation, and focus. While certainly every magazine tailors the job duties of their employees to best suit its needs, there are several basic positions that are common to most publications:

Publisher

The publisher supervises every single aspect of the magazine. The publisher determines policy and establishes the overall direction of the magazine. He or she may own the magazine, or may have been hired by the corporate ownership. Occasionally, the publisher contributes to the magazine's editorial content, but his or her duties are primarily business-based.

Editor-in-Chief

An editor-in-chief is primarily in charge of magazine content. He or she decides the theme of each edition, as well as the overall direction of the magazine. The editor-in-chief evaluates trends and delegates administrative responsibilities to the executive or managing editor.

Executive or Managing Editor

Following the guidelines established by the editor-in-chief, the executive or managing editor leads the editorial staff. Along with his or her assistants, the executive editor assigns stories to freelance or staff writers. The executive editor also attends story conferences, consults on idea or story treatments, and supervises the department editors. Most executive or managing editors today hold bachelor of arts degrees and have well-developed editing and writing skills; many attained their position by working their way up through the ranks.

Senior Editor

This is an umbrella term. Depending on the publication for which he or she works, a senior editor might write columns or special pages in each issue, or oversee specific aspects of the production process, such as copy editing.

Contributing Editor

Magazines often put contributing editors on staff as well. A contributing editor might write half a dozen major articles each year. They are specialists, experts in certain areas like cooking, sports, travel, art, music, or business. Their pieces are often popular with subscribers and the extent of their appeal often determines the fee they can command for each article.

Copy Editor

Copy editors read manuscripts and proofread articles after they have been typeset. A copy editor must have strong grammar, punctuation, and spelling skills. Assistant copy editors work with the copy editor to perfect each article. Assistant copy editor is an ideal entry-level position for college graduates looking to build a career in the magazine industry.

Production Manager

The production manager coordinates the delivery of the editorial and art portions of the magazine to the printer and supervises the printing of each issue. He or she also negotiates printing contracts and orders the color separations needed to print photographs as well as special typesetting. The production manager also sets up printing schedules, selects the appropriate paper, and conducts quality checks to ensure proper and cost-efficient magazine printing.

Art Director

One of the primary tasks of an art director is to oversee the production phase of publishing. Production is the process of assembling the art, editorial, and advertising content of a new issue. A few magazines continue to use the traditional method of pasting up pages, but most now employ sophisticated computer programs and other specialized software.

Together, the art and editorial departments strive to produce a visually appealing and readable magazine. They coordinate the completion of their separate contributions to meet preset deadlines so that the magazine can be produced and distributed to retail outlets and subscribers on schedule. In addition to these positions, there are many other people who are instrumental to the success of a magazine:

Business Manager

The business manager reports directly to the publisher on the status of the magazine's financial affairs. Strong accounting and business management skills are a must for this position. Should the publisher retire or resign, the business manager is usually considered next in line for promotion to the top job.

Advertising Manager

The advertising manager is responsible for the entire advertising department. He or she assigns accounts to sales staff, keeps records of accounts and sales, and may handle large, in-house accounts personally.

Research Director

A research director usually works with the advertising sales staff to evaluate the relationship between the magazine's readers and the advertising it publishes. It is an extremely precise field that requires strong skills in computers and statistical analysis.

Marketing or Promotion Manager

Some trade magazines have a marketing manager. His or her job is to increase the magazine's visibility and popularity, as well as to guide the development of its image in the public or business sector. His or her responsibilities may include public speaking at seminars, booth design and content at trade shows, and media releases.

Circulation Director

The circulation director monitors newsstand and subscription sales. He or she directs the circulation staff and keeps track of sales and subscribers. The circulation director may also help determine the print run (how many magazines are printed) for each issue, based on market information.

Finally, as with any other business, the magazine industry depends on people with secretarial and accounting skills as well as those who work in customer service, shipping, packing, delivery, and printing. Excellent entry-level positions exist in these areas. These jobs can sometimes lead to more prominent positions within the company.

Shipping and Receiving

Workers in shipping and receiving keep records of all production materials such as paper, inks, envelopes, strapping, labels, and boxes delivered to the publishing company. They also oversee mailings of the printed magazines. This job can lead to higher positions in distribution and circulation.

The Press Room

An apprentice in the press room repairs enormous web printing presses. He or she also learns how to justify full-color plates, ensuring that a finished magazine prints accurately and is attractive to the eye. Very possibly, the company might also print in-house a quantity of the promotional materials distributed to readers and newsstands. In this case, an apprentice would also gain experience operating offset presses as well.

Accounting

Many magazine publishing companies have in-house accounting departments. They handle accounts payable and receivable as well as payroll and benefits. While a degree in accounting might be necessary for upper-level positions, many entry-level jobs involving data entry, spreadsheet development, and elementary bookkeeping require less formal education. Starting as a trainee, you could advance to the position of department supervisor, head of accounting, or office manager, and eventually become the publisher.

Working in the press room requires highly technical skills.

Customer Service

Customer service representatives answer telephone calls from subscribers and clients. Some callers might want to place classified advertisements or inquire about their subscription. Positions such as these can evolve into promotions to the advertising sales and the circulation and subscription departments.

Secretarial

No business, magazine publishing included, operates smoothly without secretarial help. These secretarial or assisting positions are a marvelous way to learn about the magazine publishing business using those skills you may have already developed, such as keyboarding, interpersonal communications, telephone usage, organization, follow-up, teamwork, and problem solving.

What Lies Ahead

You are probably wondering what the magazine career field will look like by the time you graduate from college. Mark Hall, an instructor in the telecommunications program at Butte College in Oroville, California, shares one insider's perspective. He teaches courses in career preparation for media majors seeking jobs in print, broadcasting, film, and the Internet. According to Hall, "Students in the cyber future will need the same reading, writing, and editing skills they need today.

However, they will also need to be able to use a wide variety of writing, design, and editing software."

Hall urges students interested in a magazine career to gain as much hands-on experience as possible in order to prepare for a rapidly changing media landscape. He suggests working with high school and college publications or finding a part-time position with a local newspaper.

One thing is certain: Magazine publishing offers a wide range of career possibilities to explore. In the following chapters, we will take a closer look at each aspect of magazine publishing. You will hear from professionals working in the field what it is like to be an editor, an advertising director, or a production manager and you will learn what it takes to achieve your goal—a career in magazines.

The Core:
Publishers and Editors

2

A magazine's publisher oversees financial and corporate matters, including advertising, distribution, staffing, accounting, and payroll. Its editors focus on the magazine's content, design, and scope. Small magazines may have only one publisher who works with one or two editors. The publisher of a major magazine frequently has several associates who oversee dozens, or perhaps hundreds of editors in offices spread throughout the country or worldwide. Regardless of the number of editors a magazine publishing company employs, or the size of the publisher's staff, these two upper-level divisions form the core of any magazine.

The Role of the Publisher

The publisher oversees all business aspects of magazine operations. The publisher interfaces with owners, boards of directors, and the editorial staff. Department heads report directly to the publisher on the progress of their respective offices. As you may have already guessed, most publishers have years of experience working for magazines. Publishers need to know a lot about writing, editing, accounting, distribution, production, and managing.

The Editor's Role

Editors oversee the creative side of magazine publishing. They spend hours in meetings, planning the contents of each issue. They work well in advance of the magazine's distribution date, which means they must be aware not only of current trends but also of developing ones. Editors often determine themes up to one year in advance for holiday or special issues. After developing the basic outline for an issue, editors decide what articles to assign to staff or freelance writers. The editors of each division also select the photographs and artwork to complement the articles.

As writers submit their articles, the editors organize and sometimes even rewrite them as the theme of each issue evolves. Even though the editors may have started working on an issue as early as six months in advance of their deadline, they often spend many extra hours right before deadline bringing the issue into perfect balance.

Editors are responsible for making sure that each issue is attractive and readable. They maintain the stylistic integrity of the publication. They work closely with the publisher, who may announce changes in the magazine's slant—the way the magazine presents different topics—or other policy changes decided upon by the company's board of directors.

Duties are numerous, varied, and sometimes unpredictable. Good magazine editors are resourceful, persistent, flexible, and creative. They also work closely with the sales, art, and production departments to ensure that all the different components of an issue complement each other and are presented in a seamless, readable manner.

Most magazines focus on a particular topic, such as fashion, news, or sports, and the editors must know the latest trends in that field. Current topics of interest in the magazine's specialty area dictate what will appear in a magazine. In some cases, the magazines themselves set trends by generating interest in their subject area.

Editing is intellectually stimulating work that might include investigative research in fields such as politics, history, and business. Editors are responsible for the accuracy and objectivity of their work. Magazine editors must exercise good judgment; the opinions, editorials, or essays they choose to print can influence a large number of readers.

Depending on the size of the magazine, editors may specialize in a particular area. For instance, a fashion magazine may have a beauty editor, a features editor, a short story editor, and a fashion editor. Each editor may be responsible for setting a budget for his or her department, and negotiating contracts with freelance writers, photographers, and artists.

Each editor is responsible for acquiring, proofing, rewriting, and sometimes writing articles for their section. They must also work closely with each other to produce a cohesive issue. After determining an issue's focus, the editor assigns articles to writers and photographers. The editor supervises copy editors, assistant editors, fact checkers, researchers, and editorial assistants as they contribute their skills to the formation of each article.

Editing is intellectually stimulating and influential work.

Once an article is submitted, the magazine editor reviews the material, checking it for clarity, brevity, and audience appeal. Frequently, the editor will edit the text in order to highlight particular items. Sometimes the editor writes an editorial to stimulate discussion or influence public opinion. The editor may also choose to write articles on topics which he or she finds particularly interesting.

Editors must have an ear for the written word as well as an impeccable knowledge of grammar, spelling, punctuation, and word usage. They must also be organized, objective, and possess the necessary managerial skills to oversee their department and ensure that articles flow smoothly from editorial through production.

Editorial Assistant

Editorial assistants learn on the job what life as an editor is like. They also participate in training seminars, and often go back to school for specialty classes that enhance their skills. While these positions are largely administrative, many people work their way up. All entry-level positions in magazine publishing, such as editorial assistant or intern, require a working knowledge of keyboarding and word processing, as well as a solid command of grammar, punctuation, and spelling. Since deadlines are a fact of magazine life, the ability to work well under pressure is a must in magazine publishing. Punctuality, commitment, organization, and resourcefulness are key characteristics of a highly effective editorial assistant.

Succeeding as a Magazine Editor

To successfully build a career as a magazine editor, you will need at least a bachelor of arts degree; common majors are English, journalism, communications, or literature. If you have already narrowed down your field of interest to editing magazines, you should pursue a liberal arts major with a minor in your chosen field of expertise.

Most colleges and universities offer courses in magazine design, writing, editing, and photography. Related courses might include newspaper and book editing. If you did not gain experience working on a high school newspaper, these courses will help broaden your knowledge and increase your value to a prospective employer.

Jerold K. Footlick, a *Newsweek* editor for twenty years, advises, "I firmly believe that those who want a career in magazine publishing must start focusing on the skills they'll need as early as their freshman year in high school." He also believes in developing a broad base of knowledge. "As far as a college major is concerned, I recommend liberal arts, with a minor in journalism. It's important to know how to write. But it's even more important to know at least the fundamentals on a diversity of subjects. For example, if a job applicant seeks an editorial position with a magazine that focuses on world economy, it would help to know world history, geography, politics, and economics as well as how to edit and write."

Footlick, a finalist for the Pulitzer Prize in civil rights coverage, managed several different news departments during his career at *Newsweek*. "The more you know about everything that goes on around you, the more valuable you will be to your publisher and managing editor," he stresses. "It may sound trite, but the best thing an aspiring writer or editor can do, starting right now, is read, read, read," he stresses.

"Read all sorts of magazines. Study them, analyze how each is composed and what types of art editors have selected to illustrate the articles. Know what goes into a magazine from personal observation. Do that, and you'll develop an instinctive feel for the profession."

He believes that high school students can gain experience in the skills necessary for good magazine editing by working on their school newspaper or literary magazine. He also suggests starting a newsletter or magazine about any topic or hobby you find of great interest. Any experience writing, editing, and putting copy together to produce a publication is invaluable to the aspiring magazine editor.

Internships are sometimes available to students during their last two years of college. Generally, they are summer programs that offer students hands-on experience. Students should take advantage of these offers, especially if they have had little or no editing experience. Journalism professors and career counselors will often recommend exceptional students for internships. Publications often hire their interns full time after they graduate.

Competition is fierce for these jobs. Applicants for magazine editing positions must prepare cover letters and résumés with care. These documents are the first examples of the applicant's work, and will be judged accordingly. Along with the résumé, applicants should include a clip file of articles they have written or edited. This should be limited to six to eight examples reflecting the applicant's most outstanding work. Experience and internships should be highlighted.

Developing personal interests and hobbies compatible with magazine publishing can help, too. Perhaps you love to write fact or fiction about all kinds of things. Maybe you enjoy taking your camera everywhere you go just in case something catches your eye or fires your imagination. Those are skills and interests that can enhance your career as a magazine editor.

Working as an Editor

An editor's job description can vary, depending on the size, scope, and focus of a magazine. A mid-size special interest publication with a circulation of about 350,000 may employ an editorial staff of twelve: editor-in-chief, executive editor, managing editor, art director, four associate editors, one production manager, one editorial assistant, one assistant to the art director, and one clerical person to enter copy. The editors must be able to work as a team in a large publishing company.

An editor for a smaller magazine might hire writers, oversee production, coordinate advertising with layout, and develop strategies for increasing subscriptions. Here, again, it is important for editors to be flexible, creative, and resourceful when carrying an especially heavy workload. Editors work primarily indoors, in an office, cell, or work pool. They spend most of their time working on computers at their desks or talking on the telephone. They also constantly interact with the publisher and editorial support staff, both informally and during meetings.

There is little or no privacy in most editorial departments and they are often short on space and comfort.

Editors must have the ability to concentrate under tight deadlines and the patience to accommodate many interruptions.

Managing and senior editors may have private offices while the rest of the editorial staff works at desks in small cells or in a newsroom. An editor must develop the ability to concentrate in adverse conditions, and to deal with interruptions in a calm, professional manner.

Along with the day-to-day challenges, approaching issue deadlines may require an editor to work overtime, adding many more hours to what is commonly a fifty-hour workweek. As you can see, editorial positions are not necessarily glamorous. But the job does have perks. Salaries typically range from $25,000 to $43,000 for experienced editors. Editorial assistants can expect salaries of $20,000 to $28,000. Senior editors of major circulation magazines can earn more than $75,000 annually. They sometimes supplement their income by writing freelance pieces.

Advancement in magazine editing can happen rapidly. People in publishing change jobs constantly, seeking upper-level positions inside and outside of their company. As your experience increases, so will your prospects for a higher-level, better-paying position.

The majority of magazine editors work their way up through the ranks. Most of them started as interns, editorial assistants, writers, or copy editors. There are assistant, associate, senior, and managing editors. Because a magazine editor's position requires supervising the editorial staff, some managerial experience is helpful.

"I guess you could say I took a circuitous route," says Ellen Payne, managing editor of *Glamour*, a Condé Nast publication. "I have a degree with an emphasis on Latin American literature from a school that stressed writing. In 1985, I went to work as an editorial assistant for a motorcycle magazine in Los Angeles. It was small. I believe small operations are a good place to start, because you learn about every aspect of editing."

Payne also notes that she advanced rapidly, from working as an editorial assistant to managing editor. She became managing editor of a photography magazine eighteen months later. She then worked for many years at home as a freelance editor and writer while raising her children. Later, Payne and her family moved to New York, where she became managing editor of *Cosmopolitan*. From there, she moved to *Glamour*.

Looking back, Payne is amazed at how quickly she moved up in the field, becoming managing editor at *Glamour* after being in New York for three-and-a-half years. The experience gives her a special perspective. "Small publishers are great places to get started," Payne observes. "On the other hand, if an applicant can get a foot in the door at Condé Nast, he or she is set for life."

Still, Payne stresses that there is nothing wrong with working out of your home. Being at home gives editors more scheduling flexibility. Further, continuing to work enables freelance editors to network so that they can more easily find excellent positions when they are ready to re-enter the workforce. In fact, she adds, for men and women alike, freelance editing is an alternative way to be involved in magazine publishing and also raise a family. "Networking is important, though," Payne says. "Keeping your finger on the pulse of publishing through many magazine contacts is a good way to learn about opportunities for future positions."

Openings at the highest levels of editing are infrequent. Many top editors stay in their positions for ten years or longer. Lower-level editors often must advance their careers by finding higher-paying positions at other companies.

Magazine publishing is a dynamic industry. It constantly changes. And new magazines are launched every day, focusing mostly on special interests. There are an increasing number of opportunities for editorial positions at these magazines, if your educational background matches the magazine's specialty. As in many fields, the competition for jobs is fierce.

The time to start planning for these exciting, rewarding careers is right now. Payne believes that internships are one of the best ways to begin. "You can intern as early as in your senior year in high school." Payne adds, "The contacts you make through internships make excellent references. And, you never know what you'll learn. By exploring editing, art, fashion, advertising, and other magazine elements, you will find what you like best."

The Written Word: In-House and Freelance

Writing is one of the most exciting and demanding careers in the magazine publishing field. Publishers hire both in-house (or staff) writers and freelance writers. Staff writers are full-time magazine employees. They write primarily departmental pieces or work that relates to the magazine's focus. Publishers also use freelance writers who typically develop and produce articles from a home office for any number of employers.

In-House

Most magazine writers get their start as in-house or staff authors. Staff writers have the security of a steady income and benefits. Staff writers also work in a stimulating environment that offers hands-on experience. They can remain fairly sure that the editor-in-chief will publish their articles. Entry-level writers may also begin to edit as they gain more work experience.

Freelance

While a few magazines are written entirely in-house, the vast majority rely on freelance writers to fill their pages with well-written, thoroughly researched articles that inform and entertain readers. Skim through *Writer's Market*, one of the foremost resource books for freelance writers, and you will discover under each magazine entry the percentage of freelance material it publishes. These percentages range from as low as 5 percent to 100 percent.

Payment for freelance articles varies just as widely, from pennies a word to more than $1,000 for an article. Literary or small publications often pay authors with copies of the issue instead of money. Why should you write for them? Because demonstrating that your work is worthy of being published can open doors; published articles validate your writing skills to editors.

Some magazines pay freelance writers on acceptance, meaning the writer is paid when the magazine receives the article and agrees to publish it. Other magazines pay on publication, when the article actually appears in an issue. This can be as long as a year after a magazine's editorial staff accepts it.

How do you make a living as a freelance writer? Not easily. The American Society of Journalists and Authors conducted a survey of 500 established freelance writers. What they learned about median income was discouraging. The average freelance writer surveyed made less than $10,000 annually. Columbia University conducted a similar study of people who had written at least one book, and found the average annual income from freelance writing was $4,775. As 20-year *Newsweek* veteran editor, Jerold K. Footlick, warns, "There's nothing wrong with working as a free-lance writer. Just don't quit your day job."

Still, there are success stories. Stephen King published several short stories in magazines before his first best seller, *Carrie*, cemented his career. King continued to contribute short stories to magazines, including "The Raft" and "Mrs. Todd's Shortcut." The market for nonfiction magazine articles is almost double that for fiction. Once you find your "niche" and specialize in a particular field or subject, such as travel, food, sports, fashion, entertainment, or gardening, you can build a career in freelance writing that is every bit as satisfying, if not quite as profitable, as King's.

Of course, you can write both fiction and nonfiction, and you do not have to focus on one subject. The field of freelance writing is broad and inviting. But you do need to develop a network of contacts and prove to magazine editors how serious you are about making freelance writing your life's work. You also need to be a self-starter. Freelance writers work on their own, without the support and camaraderie of a team of writers and editors.

The Best of Both Worlds

Jeff Csatari is a successful magazine writer and editor. His career path includes both freelance and staff experience. Since graduating from Trenton State College in New Jersey in 1983, Csatari's career has taken him on an exciting and fulfilling journey across America and around the world. "I majored in English, and minored in journalism and professional writing. I was editor of the school magazine, *Gumption*, and worked regularly for the school newspaper, *The Signal*."

Magazine writers can be both in-house, or on staff, and freelance

A college varsity football player, Csatari also worked as a sports stringer, or freelance reporter, at the *Trenton Times*, and covered sports part-time for the *Bucks County Courier Times*. During the two years after he graduated from Trenton State, Csatari worked as diamond editor for a jewelry trade magazine in New York. "I traveled around the world covering the diamond industry," Csatari explains.

From the diamond industry, Csatari moved to Dallas, Texas, and went to work as a features editor at *Boys' Life*, a magazine published by the Boy Scouts of America. "I held that position for six years and loved every minute of it." Csatari adds, "I handled all the departments, and I also wrote most of the outdoor adventure features."

Csatari left *Boys' Life* to join the staff of *Men's Health* magazine in Emmaus, Pennsylvania. From 1992 to 1996, Csatari's responsibilities included writing, assigning articles to freelance writers, and editing features and front-of-the-book departments, including the popular "Malegrams" section. Csatari notes, "My feature, 'The Personal Trainer From Hell,' was nominated for a National Magazine Award by the American Society of Magazine Editors in 1996."

For the next two years, Csatari worked as launch editor of *Verge*. "It was a magazine about new technology for young men, published by the Times Mirror Magazines in New York," Csatari recalls. "It was an offshoot of *Popular Science* magazine. I launched it as a contract [or freelance editor] before becoming a staff member. We produced seven issues before the company folded the magazine." Following the closing of *Verge*, Csatari worked as a deputy editor at *Men's Journal*, published by Wenner Media. He then returned to *Men's Health*, where he is now launching editor of a spin-off magazine targeted at teens.

Having both freelance and staff writing experience, Csatari has access to the best and worst of both worlds. "The best advice I can give is to read as much as you can of as many types of writing as you can," Csatari says. "Work for your school newspaper or string for a professional paper."

Csatari adds that he believes newspaper reporting is great training for any type of writing career. "It teaches you to get the information correctly, to get it fast, and to write it quickly. Having to write fifteen inches of copy on an overtime high school basketball game in ten minutes, and then dictate it to my editor over the phone, was one of the greatest on-the-job lessons I've ever learned. Newspapering also teaches you to write tight."

Csatari also contends, "While some people will no doubt disagree, I think adding an M.B.A., or some other graduate degree to your J-degree is much smarter than getting a master's in journalism." Finally, Csatari advises that if you want to freelance, write a couple of short pieces for free or "on speculation" to establish a relationship with an editor.

"Well done, those freebie assignments will blossom into many, many more." Csatari concludes, "Clips mean a lot."

Becoming a Writer

"Holly G. Miller is my 'real' name, although I've used many pen names during my career for various reasons," recalls this journalist and freelance writer. "The oddest is Leslie Holden, used for a series of romance novels I wrote with a friend, a guy named Dennis Hensley. We

Journalists surround activist Al Sharpton at a rally in Brooklyn, New York. Sometimes reporters must be aggressive to get a story.

combined our names and came up with Leslie Holden. The translation: it's Les of a Lie to admit we're Hol and Den. Get it?"

Miller has a bachelor of arts degree in journalism and English from Indiana University. She returned to college and received her M.A. from Ball State University. "I started my writing career at a newspaper as a police and city hall reporter," Miller remembers. "I worked my way through the chairs in the features department and ended up as managing editor. After six years, I applied to *The Saturday Evening Post* and was hired as senior editor."

Miller's affiliation with the *Post* is still intact after a twenty-three-year working relationship. Miller has spent most of that time working from her home, about forty-five miles from the *Post*'s headquarters in Indianapolis. She also worked on-staff at *The Country Gentleman*. There, she used the byline "H.G. Miller" because the publisher believed all staff members should be men.

Miller then went on to work as both a consulting and contributing editor for *Clarity* magazine, whose final issue printed in June 2000. Miller reflects on her vast and varied writing career. "I should tell you I've also worked as a public relations generalist and speechwriter for General Motors and have taught full-time at Anderson University, as well as having written several books." Miller adds, "I absolutely love the field of writing and have wanted to explore every aspect. My favorite, however, is writing for magazines."

She prefers magazine writing because she enjoys the immediacy of seeing her work in monthly publications. She also appreciates the flexibility writing for a magazine offers. "I much prefer magazines to newspapers, because the articles can be more thoughtful and in-depth." Miller adds, "Still, my years in newspaper journalism gave me great training as far as meeting deadlines, conducting interviews, and working FAST."

Miller points out that although she has progressed from one area of writing to another, she has never truly left any of them behind. "I still do freelance public relations writing, still write for myriad magazines, still teach, still write an occasional book." According to Miller, "If you develop strong skills, you have the flexibility to explore many careers. I never thought I'd end up in magazines, yet that became an option." Looking back, Miller adds that she is glad she pursued that extra degree because it allowed her to teach others in her field.

In-House or Freelance?

Having worked in both freelance and in-house writer positions, Miller has an informed perspective on the editorial process. "Working on-staff for a magazine was a real eye-opener," Miller recalls. "Previously, I had worked at a newspaper and freelanced on the side. When I would get rejection slips, I never knew why. So, once on the other side of the magazine editor's desk, I learned some of the reasons manuscripts are returned."

"Often, it's because the material falls short quality-wise," Miller says. "But it's also very likely the magazine has too large an inventory of material and cannot add to it. Or, the editors already have a similar project in the works. Sometimes, the writing is exceptional, but the author hasn't targeted it to the publication's unique demographics."

"I also learned that magazine journalism is not all glamour," Miller continues. "Yes, I got to travel but I also got to open tons of slush [unsolicited manuscripts], learned to nit-pick over misplaced commas, and had to worry about legal matters, personnel problems, and other dilemmas."

"Too often, outsiders only see the exciting side of magazine writing," Miller explains. "There can be a downside to almost every assignment, no matter how wonderful it may seem. For example, I was assigned to go to Norway to write an advance story on the Winter Olympic Games. Now, that was fun! But I also had to write and edit ho-hum articles about politicians I didn't like, and celebrities that didn't always deserve the public's favor."

The staff writing and editing experience was a real education. Miller contributed to overall magazine content, assigned stories to writers, and anxiously awaited their first drafts. "I carefully evaluated the drafts and sent them back for revisions," Miller says of the process. "That was sometimes the most difficult part if the author had an inflated ego." Miller says she also learned the importance of striving for perfection. After all, if a mistake slips by, a spelling error, for example, the mistake is public. "Some half-million people will spot it, and many of them delight in dashing off letters pointing out our errors," Miller says.

Freelancing is Miller's personal preference. At any given time, she might be working on four to five articles simultaneously. The articles might discuss any number of topics and be in differing stages of development. For Miller, freelance writing provides the variety that she believes is the spice of life. Miller also stresses, "I certainly don't just get to write what I want to write. In fact, I often am assigned articles that don't interest me at all. But I love working in sweats, sometimes very late at night, in my home office with my cats purring on the floor next to my feet."

Miller cautions that some misperceptions regarding freelance writing do exist. She stresses, "It's not for the newcomer in the writing business. You only freelance after you have built up a name and can be assured of work. Also, many editors think if you work at home, then you're always at the office. They call night and day, and on weekends."

Miller also reminds prospective freelance writers, "You'll get very hungry if you limit yourself to what YOU want to write. Your passion may be short fiction or poetry or first-person essays, but the truth is, that isn't what sells."

Miller believes that authors can survive economically writing on a strictly freelance basis, but she admits it is not easy. She recalls, "The first article I ever offered to an editor was accepted. I got a check for $100 almost immediately. I

It takes many years of writing experience to be a successful freelance writer.

thought, 'Wow, this is easy! I think I'll quit my newspaper job, drop out of grad school, and stay home to churn out a couple of these a week.' Good thing I didn't. A full year passed before I made another sale."

Education and Experience

If you are interested in magazine writing, Miller recommends attending and graduating from college. "One of my mentors once taught me, 'Always get one more degree than you think you need.' It was great advice." Currently, Miller teaches a magazine writing class at Ball State, a large state university, as well as a class at a small private college, Anderson University.

"I see strengths in both programs, so pick the school that has the best writing major and an environment which is comfortable for you." Miller suggests, "Do internships. When you go looking for a job, the editor will want to see your portfolio, not your grade transcript." The fact that you hold a degree is a given; it is what you can offer beyond that which is important.

"Experience is great. Clips are a necessity. Letters of recommendation from internship supervisors are good, too," Miller says. "While on campus—or in high school, for that matter—accumulate as many different experiences as you can. Work on the newspaper, the yearbook staff, or at the campus radio station."

As you can see, the field of magazine writing offers many opportunities. The trick is to take the advice of these experienced writers and start now. Talk to your school's career counselor about classes offered at your high school that will best prepare you for college journalism courses. Also, try contacting junior college or university career counselors as well. They can provide information about programs and internships available in your community.

Image Is Everything:
Graphics
and Photography

As you approach the magazine shelves in the public library, you see a vivid photograph surrounded by a golden yellow border. You do not need to read the cover to recognize the magazine as *National Geographic*. Why? Because *National Geographic* magazine has featured that distinctive cover design for as long as most people can remember.

In fact, there are a number of magazines you could recognize without reading a word on the cover. *Time, Newsweek, Life, People, Vogue, Tiger Beat,* and many others rely on this instant recognition. This design is called "format." The consistency of the format enables readers to spot their favorite magazines, regardless of how or where they are displayed. Typically, a magazine's format is the product of intensive marketing, research, and creative development.

Each magazine's format is designed to be as unique as an individual's fingerprint. While elements of each issue may vary subtly, the overall look of the magazine remains the same, issue after issue. Magazine publishers rarely change a magazine's format abruptly. If a change occurs, it is usually because the publishing team believes that a magazine needs a fresh image to boost sales and remain competitive.

When you hear the term "graphics," you may think only of artwork. In the magazine publishing world, graphics encompasses not only art but also design details such as style of type, the layout of each page, where art or photography is placed on that page, or the spacing between columns of type. In other words, graphics encompasses not only the artwork inside but also the visual design of the magazine.

Working as a Graphic Designer

Often, those who work in the graphics department of a magazine publishing company do more than design the in-house magazines. For example, Faith Berven works as an associate art director for Meredith Corporation in Des Moines, Iowa, which publishes *Midwest Living* magazine.

"I've been with Meredith for a total of twenty-six years... I started at Meredith in the books department as a graphic designer immediately after graduating from Iowa State University with a bachelor of arts degree in graphic design." Berven says she designed books for eight years, then went back to college for two more years to earn her master of arts degree in fine art. After completing her master's, Berven returned to Meredith as an associate design director in a department within the company called Meredith Publishing Services.

Here, Berven helped design a fashion magazine for *Motherhood Maternity*; dog and cat magazines for the Iams Pet Food Company; holiday magazines for Hallmark;

cookbooks for Kraft; and a brochure for Sherwin Williams Paints, just to name a few. "I moved to *Midwest Living* magazine about three years ago," Berven adds. "My responsibilities at *Midwest Living* include the design and layout of assigned portions of the magazine, art directing photography and illustration, proofing the stories as they go through the art and editorial departments, photoediting film, color-correcting proofs, and doing press checks to obtain the best color possible when our magazine is running on the press."

The Impact of Technology

Berven notes that the design and production process has changed greatly since she started at Meredith. "Originally, layout was done on boards of heavy paper with black and white position stats of the photography, drawn boxes to indicate blocks of copy, and headline type that had either been roughed in by pencil or typeset and pasted down." Berven continues, "After the design had been approved, we then did final 'paste-up' with actual type pasted down in position on the boards."

Everything Meredith does in publishing today is on computer. Berven sees the computer as a great tool. "It's much faster and easier to make changes, and being able to see those changes immediately is wonderful." She adds, "Most of my working day is spent on the computer designing the stories I've been assigned."

Berven admits that keeping her designs fresh and related to each story can be a challenge. "The hardest part can be starting something new, facing that blank sheet of paper." Gracefully combining all aspects of an article can also prove tricky.

Graphic designers work with art, type, layout, and photography.

"While some days are spent primarily on production aspects of my job, such as proofing color or type, on other days I'm busy with photography sessions in the studio or, sometimes, on location," Berven says. "There are often meetings to discuss photo-planning or upcoming stories and layouts that I have to attend as well." Berven enjoys working with the different photographers and illustrators who bring their talents to *Midwest Living* assignments.

Berven also delights in her coworkers. "Everyone is very creative and talented, and brings his or her own unique talent to the magazine." Berven comments further, "I also enjoy being able to work on a quality magazine for which I am able to be involved from the beginning of a story through the entire production of the piece. I find it very satisfying to feel that I have contributed to the final look of an issue of *Midwest Living.*"

Training

If you are interested in the field of graphic design, Berven suggests exploring all aspects of the field, including publication design, Web site design for e-zines, and design in video and broadcasting. "I believe there are more avenues to explore now than ever before." She suggests, "If indeed magazine publishing is the area in which you are interested, look at the wide range of publications out there and keep your eye on design trends."

Berven recommends joining the staff of your high school yearbook or school paper in order to gain hands-on experience. Art, computer, and photography classes will also foster your future in magazine design and graphics. She also encourages potential graphic designers to explore the Internet in search of fun Web sites and to join a college graphic design club.

Overall, she stresses the importance of doing things that inspire your creativity. "If this is the profession of your choice, you must be creative. You must also be able to take criticism, [and] be conscientious about deadlines. I think an ability to relate and work well with people really helps, too. After all, we're talking about a profession in communications. Also, an understanding and knowledge of the computer is essential these days."

According to Berven, in order to successfully obtain an entry-level position at a magazine, you will need a bachelor of fine arts degree in graphic design or a degree from a good technical institute that offers graphic design courses. She advises, "While you are still in school, you should start putting together a portfolio of your work consisting of class assignments which you feel were especially successful. Even better would be an actual printed piece to which you contributed."

Berven also suggests finding an internship at a printing company, for example, so you can gain the experience and references needed to acquire a position in magazine graphics. Finally, Berven observes, "Being a graphic designer can be demanding, and even frustrating, but you are rewarded with a real sense of fun and creativity. I am very happy with my choice in careers."

Photography

Photographs are a key element of magazines. Very few magazines publish without photos. Strong, colorful photographs enhance the articles. Indeed, a picture often paints a thousand words. In fact, some popular magazines use photography almost exclusively to tell their stories.

Photographers are always in demand—very few magazines publish without photos.

The 1999 edition of *Writer's Market* characterizes *Life*—formerly a monthly magazine, now published occasionally as showing "the world through the power of pictures." To do this successfully, *Life*'s staff has cultivated an enormous group of freelance photographers from around the world.

Vivette Porges describes her work in the past as an associate picture editor for *Life*. "Very often, picture editors serve as the first viewers of the photography that will eventually be published in a magazine. I see photographers' unsolicited or solicited photo stories and story ideas continuously."

Porges and a team of staff members choose the photographers for each assignment. "Through discussion of the story with the editors and creative director, the final choice of photographer will be decided." Porges adds, "I do the first photo edit of a story, and follow through the production of it with the photographer, editor, and designer." *Life* magazine has only one professional photographer on contract. Freelance photographers shoot most of the photos that you see in *Life*.

Develop Style

The best thing you can do, right now, if you're interested in a career in magazine photography, is to not only learn the mechanics of photography, but also study the styles of various photographers. Every photographer develops a style that distinguishes his or her work.

Many photographers specialize, focusing on a particular area such as sports, travel, wildlife, politics, etc. Whether a specialist or a generalist, the successful photographer has a sound working knowledge of photographic equipment and what it can do. After all, there is no second chance to take a once-in-a-lifetime picture.

Porges advises aspiring photographers to "read books on photography. Look through old and current magazines to get familiarized with what you see. Get involved in extracurricular activities that revolve around photography. If it's the only way to get in the door, volunteer."

Interning at the photo department of your local newspaper, a magazine, or in a photographer's studio will help you learn first-hand about photography. "Offering to assist a photographer whose work you admire, even for low or no pay, is a great way to gain entry into the field," Porges adds. "Career-focused part-time work is a plus for high school students and will give you a realistic understanding of the workplace before college." These jobs can become stepping-stones to better job positions and higher pay.

"Tagging along to lend a hand at a shoot and willingness to help out is very important," Porges advises. "Being able to scan photographs and having computer skills is also a plus. Ask questions and be curious!" Lastly, Porges cautions, "patience is essential because one's goals aren't always reached as quickly or exactly as one hopes."

Freelance Photography

Freelance photographers, like freelance writers, are professionals who work on their own, contributing to any number of magazines. Susan Watts is a professional photographer who works on a freelance basis for *Life* magazine. "I am actually a staff photographer at the New York *Daily News*," Watts says. "I work for *Life* during my vacation time from the *News*."

Watts graduated from New York University in 1991 with a bachelor of fine arts in film. "I became interested in still photography as I learned filmmaking. I realized it was where I wanted my career to go." Watts adds, "I freelanced for two years at the *Daily News* before they hired me on staff in 1995. I have been freelancing at *Life* since 1992."

Watts' workday varies widely. Some days she shoots five assignments while on others she might spend the whole day photographing children playing in a park. "I do travel," Watts notes. "I recently came back from Miami, where I was covering the Elian Gonzalez story. I went to Honduras to cover the aftermath of Hurricane Mitch for *Life* magazine. I love to shoot everything. Virtually all situations offer opportunities for dramatic and beautiful moments."

Photojournalism can be both dangerous and exhilarating.

What you can do right now, Watts advises, is to learn your craft and stay focused on your goals. "Decide what kind of photographer you are," she adds. "A newspaper (or magazine) photographer? A portrait photographer? An architectural photographer? Put together a strong portfolio. "And keep shooting, shooting, shooting."

Photojournalism

Photojournalism is the art of telling stories through the use of photography. Andrew Lichtenstein is a professional freelance photographer who also works on assignment for *Life* magazine. He became interested in photojournalism because he has always been obsessed with history. "I can watch allied propaganda movies of World War II for days at a time," Lichtenstein admits. "I found photography to be a relatively easy and quick way to get inside all the history books I was reading. Now I can witness events for myself."

Lichtenstein feels that there are many ways to become a photojournalist. "No narrow photography education is necessary for success," he explains. "It will always help to be well-read on a variety of subjects that have nothing to do with photography."

He sees photography as one of the few "arts" that retain a practical purpose. "In my case, pictures illustrate articles in magazines," Lichtenstein says. "I enjoy that specific craftsman-like role. Unlike most dancers or painters or poets, I have found it possible to pursue an independent art and pay the rent, essentially without ever getting a job. Not bad!"

Lichtenstein believes you should be open to all kinds of photography. "Feel your way" toward what you like best. Photojournalism is just one of the many possible choices. Finally, Lichtenstein urges aspiring photographers to consider any volunteer work a free education. "For the journalists, I would advise never to be afraid to work for free in the beginning. Every town or city has small, community-based publications. The assignments you can receive from them are the same you might be doing in the future for large magazines. Jump into the field by really doing it." He concludes, "You will learn more than any school could ever teach you."

As these professionals have illustrated, working in the fields of design and photography can be fun and challenging. Both require creativity, technical skills, and discipline. As a magazine designer or contributing photographer, you can become a visual storyteller.

Putting the Pieces Together: Production

When the articles, photography, artwork, and advertising portions of a magazine are ready for publication, the production department prepares the magazine for the press. Picture the magazine at this point as a large shipping box. The label might read, "Contents: twenty-one feature articles, twelve monthly columns, fifteen regular features, 142 photographs, twenty-seven pieces of custom-assigned artwork, 583 advertisements of varying sizes, masthead, table of contents. Assembly required."

The production department receives this "box," along with a set of instructions called a "dummy" or rough layout. These layouts indicate where to place the ads, artwork, and photographs. The layout also notes where to "jump" the articles, indicating the pages on which an article starts and the pages toward the back of the magazine where the article continues. Following these guidelines, the production staff builds the magazine, page by page.

Until relatively recently, magazine pages were key-lined. A board was taped onto a drawing board, and the typeset articles, photographs, artwork, and advertisements were pasted down onto it either with rubber cement or hot wax. This work was extremely labor-intensive. The materials attached to the boards had to be carefully lined up and cleaned of any glue or wax residue to ensure the page was perfect and "camera-ready." Not surprisingly, "paste-up" is another common term for this process. The board was then photographed. From the negative of this photograph, a zinc or plastic plate was produced. This plate was then attached to the press rollers and the magazine was printed.

Today, most production departments use computers and highly sophisticated software instead. Often software is customized to more efficiently produce magazines. After proofreading, the typeset articles are downloaded directly into computer generated pages. Artwork and photographs are positioned using digital imaging, or a scanner that translates images into digital computer code.

As you can imagine, the new computer-aided process is considerably faster and the results are often more precise. Currently in the field of magazine production, computer skills are essential. Nevertheless, some traditional layout skills, such as having a "feel" for space and balance, remain vital. Listening to a professional in the production field reveals the impact of this change.

Production Director

Sean Keefe, editorial production director for several publications from Hearst Magazines, including *Country Living*, *Country Living Gardener*, and *Country Living's Healthy Living*, describes his duties. "Basically, I oversee all the editorial production. This means that I have to make sure the magazine gets put together and out the door on time."

"The production department at *Country Living* magazine consists of three people: a production associate, a production assistant, and me," Keefe says. "In terms of working environment, it is a very open group. All three of us share the work fairly equally. I have sort of a rule that I run my department by, which is that I will never give someone else a job to do that I wouldn't do myself."

However, Keefe admits that the scope of his position sometimes dictates that he delegate certain responsibilities. The duties of a production director range from supervising the printing process to negotiating printing contracts, ordering typography (typesetting for the editorial and advertising portions) and color separations, to coordinating the arrival of art and editorial pieces.

"I work with the managing editor and copy department to make sure we have copy in on time. I work with the advertising department in laying out the magazine, deciding where the ads and copy will go. I'm in constant contact with our color separator and printer to make sure we are getting them workable artwork and files on time." Keefe occasionally oversees the actual printing of the magazine, to make sure it meets color standards set by the publisher. He also works closely with the art director to prepare clean digital files that produce strong, quality color images.

Production Assistant

Production assistant is an entry-level position at *Country Living*. According to Keefe, "To apply successfully, a person needs to have strong Macintosh skills, specifically

A production assistant needs strong desktop publishing skills.

QuarkXpress, plus a good working knowledge of how magazines are developed. The candidate should expect to be tested on his or her knowledge of production processes. The test results weigh heavily in my decision to hire someone."

Keefe describes the important work his production assistant tends to. "My production assistant is in charge of the basic files. She receives layouts from the art department and copy from the copy department, and then has to put the two together electronically. She also inputs all the copy corrections electronically. The associate maintains our logs, updates me when things are late, and oversees some of the production assistant's duties."

At *Country Living*, the production assistant also works for the art department. "Although the production assistant works with me, she also has many art duties," Keefe says. "She scans all the images, creates dummy books (rough drafts of the magazine), prints copies of the layouts for presentations, helps maintain and update logs, and helps the production associate."

Production Skills

Keefe also discusses the skills needed to work in production. He agrees that computers play a big part in putting *Country Living* together. "The most obvious skill required for production is computer literacy, especially Macintosh." Keefe stresses, "The software requires expert knowledge of QuarkXpress, with strong working knowledge of Adobe PhotoShop, Adobe Illustrator, and Microsoft Excel. You'll find this is common at most magazines."

Keefe believes that strong reading and writing skills, and a working knowledge of proofreader's marks are also essential to succeed in production. "Telephone and interpersonal skills are important, too, because we have to deal with many different people on a daily basis. All the people I have working for me have college degrees. Although this is helpful, I wouldn't hesitate to interview someone without a degree if he or she had the right experience."

Keefe has a bachelor of arts degree in English, with a concentration in writing. "However, almost as important, I spent my high school and college years working for a family-owned printing business, where I learned all aspects of the printing industry, including Macintosh and various software programs."

Keefe cautions newcomers not to overlook production as a possible career choice, or as a way to get your foot in the door. "Often people looking for design jobs are reluctant to take production jobs." Keefe contends, "While working in production, you might not do much design work but you will learn the right way to produce layouts."

Keefe's own route to production editor was filled with twists and turns. "I worked for my brother's printing company for about eight years before coming to Hearst. However, I have to admit that I didn't know exactly what production was when I started here, especially since it was during a time when magazines were switching from traditional production to electronic production."

Here again, internships are a great way to gain experience. For those at the high school level, Keefe advises getting involved in school newspapers or literary magazines. "These are often done on Macs using the same software we use here in our production department." Magazines often offer internship programs in editorial departments that may provide some insight into magazine production.

The Printing Crew

Press and camera operators are also considered part of the production staff. They oversee the physical (digital or mechanical) process of printing each magazine. The number of people employed and the extent of the work done within magazine production departments varies. Some magazine publishing houses have their own in-house scanning, finishing, and printing crews.

Camera Operators

Camera operators develop special plates. These plates match finished pages of the magazine. The operators mount these plates on huge press rollers. When the magazine page is in full color, each color requires a separate plate. Camera operators may also be responsible for using scanners to separate colors in photographs and artwork before making the plates. They need to have a good working knowledge of various graphic cameras, as there are several different types. Dark room experience is a must.

Press Operators

Press operators run the presses. Their responsibilities include loading paper and mixing and measuring inks. Press operators also monitor reproduction quality and repair the press when it breaks down. The printing process requires constant vigilance and patience, plus a flair for mechanics. This type of work also demands a great deal of agility and physical strength.

Press and camera operating positions are rarely entry-level. Both require substantial experience and

Press operators run the presses and monitor production quality.

training. However, you may be able to apply for internships in these fields while in college. You may also find apprenticeships in printing companies and newspapers, available to applicants with a high school diploma or an associate's degree from a two-year community college.

You might ask community newspaper editors or publishers if you could "shadow" a press operator or camera operator for a day or two to get an on-the-job feel for what the position is really like. You may also find a printing company that is willing to hire you as an assistant. Experience in the press and production positions may eventually lead to promotion to production manager or director.

The Art of Selling: Advertising and Marketing

6

Subscriptions generate a relatively small percentage of the money needed to cover the cost of producing a magazine. Magazines rely on the marketing and advertising departments to generate revenue. Frequently, the work of these departments overlaps. Sales personnel sell not only space within the magazine, but also the magazine itself.

Jim McCormick, publisher of *Successful Farming*, the first magazine published by Meredith Corporation in 1902, describes working in his magazine's advertising and marketing departments. "First, we have employees in advertising sales." McCormick explains, "They sell advertising space to businesses with products they want to sell to farmers. It's a tough job because, when you sell advertising, you're selling a concept instead of a product. It's what we call an intangible, like insurance."

A full-page, four-color ad in *Successful Farming* costs $48,215 to run in a single issue. "We don't hand them a product such as a car, even though the ad costs more than twice what an average car costs today." McCormick adds, "We can prove that ad will reach 465,000 homes and businesses with farming connections. That's what our circulation is today. The fact that we are the largest paid-circulation farming magazine in the country helps."

Sales personnel develop promotional tools such as brochures, packages, and media kits to present or mail to prospective advertisers. They also write and produce sales literature and design rate cards with the current prices for the different ad sizes in the magazine. According to McCormick, at *Successful Farming*, "we also have a team of researchers who keep the advertising sales staff informed on what kind of readers the ads will reach."

McCormick explains where to begin your career in advertising sales. Selling mail-order classified ads is the entry-level advertising position at *Successful Farming* magazine. "These are the smaller ads at the back of the magazine that are not supported by editorial content. They cost half what the ads in the front of the magazine cost. It's a good place to begin. You'll learn about competition, for one thing, as well as accuracy and thoroughness." After working for a time in magazine classifieds, you might qualify to sell advertising in what he termed "run of book" or all of the magazine's available advertising space. You would then most likely earn a combination of salary and commission (the percentage of ad sale revenue).

Necessary Skills

In order to be successful in this area of magazine publishing, you need to develop excellent oral and writing skills in high school. McCormick insists that, "You need to be able to write concise letters and follow-up on the results. You will also be asked to do presentations for clients, which requires well-developed speaking skills." "In the publishing business," McCormick explains, "everything put into print is permanent. A strong grasp of grammar, language, sentence construction, punctuation, and spelling is essential to succeed in the advertising field." As noted earlier, "If you make a mistake, people notice." McCormick continues, "An awkwardly worded letter or misspellings in a first-contact letter make a poor impression that will be hard to overcome."

"College is helpful, with an emphasis on business, marketing, or journalism," McCormick suggests. "When we advertise for new employees, we have to write the job specifications. If we say you must have a degree, then you must—otherwise we violate the equal opportunity laws. But we can modify the specifications by adding that we'll consider those with several years' experience."

McCormick emphasizes the need for computer skills. "Computer skills are a given. Everyone here either works with a laptop or a desktop computer." He adds, "They email a lot of their communications. Many work both at the office and at home. You've got to have computer capability. That's the normal way to do business today."

You can get started in the magazine advertising and marketing field by selling advertising for your high school newspaper, newsletter, and yearbook. McCormick recommends, "Do anything related to sales while you're going through college. Sell advertising for the college's newspaper and yearbook. Work part-time or full-time selling classifieds or ads at a local newspaper. One good entry-level experience is selling for the yellow pages of your local telephone directory. Another is selling advertising for a local radio station."

Market researchers gather demographic information and then present it to magazine advertisers.

Marketing

Market researchers frequently conduct surveys to evaluate readers' changing wants and needs. Market reports not only guide advertising sales staff in their efforts to fill the magazine with ads geared towards the interests and spending habits of their readers, but they also help the editorial department develop strong feature articles and helpful columns on subjects and trends of interest.

Students often overlook marketing as a magazine career option. *Ladies Home Journal* publisher Michael Brownstein says few high school students are even aware of this aspect of magazine work. "High school students are more inclined to think of journalism in connection with magazine careers," Brownstein notes. Nevertheless, he encourages students to pursue marketing. "The best way to get started toward a job in magazine marketing is to work for an advertising agency for a few years."

That is how Brownstein began his career. While he attended Pennsylvania State University, Brownstein belonged to a marketing club. "The club brought in speakers from various large advertising agencies, who talked to us about how they solved marketing problems or maintained long-term relationships with clients. When I was in my senior year, I began giving résumés to these speakers. At one of the meetings, I was the only one to give the speaker a résumé. I got a telephone call from his agency the next day. If I hadn't done that, I don't know what I'd be doing today."

Today Brownstein oversees a nine-person marketing department. The department's mission is to evaluate how *Ladies Home Journal*, the sixth largest American magazine with a circulation of 4.1 million, is positioned in the minds of its readers and how well its sales and advertising materials support that position.

"Our slogan is 'It's just smart,'" Brownstein said. "The magazine is more about issues and less about recipes. It's the smart woman's magazine, and all of our marketing and advertising materials support that concept."

Within the marketing department of *Ladies Home Journal*, designers, promoters, and event coordinators oversee events at shopping malls and women's trade shows. The marketing department also keeps a sharp eye on the magazine's demographics. Demographics are a numerical evaluation of who reads *Ladies Home Journal* and why. Demographics research informs the marketing and advertising departments of how many people read the magazine, the median age of their readership, as well as the issues and trends important to those readers.

Marketing Coordinator

According to Brownstein, a common entry-level position in marketing departments is marketing coordinator. "The coordinator helps the marketing staff by making sure all the details of any event are covered. They work on mall events and promotions, do setup onsite, and stay in continual contact with all the people involved in any promotion or event to ensure things go smoothly."

"It's crazy," Brownstein says, "but marketing staff can come from all sorts of background education and experience, including those with English or history degrees as well as those who have already worked in marketing. What we look for are people with ambition and creativity. It helps to have an advertising or marketing background," Brownstein adds. "But a lot of them tell me that, when they attended college, they never even considered working in magazine marketing. No one says 'I'm pursuing a career in magazine marketing.'"

That was how he felt when he was in high school and college. Brownstein recalls, "My brother did have some idea of what he wanted to do. He sold advertising for the school newspaper and made a few bucks. I find we hire more people out of advertising agencies than from anywhere else. If you want to get into magazine or e-zine marketing on the Internet, start in an advertising agency."

Advertising Sales

More magazine advertising director Julie Pinkwater has a bachelor of arts degree in psychology and sociology from Boston University, has ten years' experience in an

69

advertising agency, and spent three years in marketing. Pinkwater observes that the advertising and marketing divisions interface continually to build the magazine's brand image. Pinkwater explains, "Marketing does more work in events and promotions, while sales personnel sell, but they both work together for the short-term and long-term advancement of *More* magazine."

Advertising sales representatives make sales calls, set up meetings and, most importantly, follow up on presentations and contacts. They also work on sales strategies with their colleagues. Marketing provides advertising sales support, develops presentations, and works with sales on consistent brand recognition. "While marketing personnel generally spend 80 percent of their time in the office, sales staff work days are about fifty-fifty," Pinkwater says.

"Every magazine advertising department is different. But they are all lively, fun, and inspiring places to work. It's an exciting field, where people are proud of their accomplishments and work with passion. We work hard and play hard."

According to Pinkwater, to be successful in magazine advertising sales, "you have to be intelligent, tenacious, and have well-developed organizational skills. You also should be able to develop interpersonal relationships, and be a stickler on follow-up." Pinkwater notes, "Working in advertising sales is somewhat like owning your own little business. You will be expected to take responsibility for your actions, and to be accountable for maintaining good relationships with clients."

Pinkwater argues that it is more difficult to obtain a position in advertising than in marketing. She suggests starting at an advertising agency. College is a must as well. She suggests, "From there, you might go to a trade magazine to get your feet wet." Pinkwater also stresses that the very best way to break into this exciting, challenging field is through internships. Many magazine publishing companies offer internships through regional colleges and vocational schools. "If you could underline this advice and print it in bold type, please do. I could repeat this ten million times, and it wouldn't be enough. Internships are the most valuable aspect of a successful application. We don't look at grades. We want to see how you used your summers. And it doesn't matter if you have completed several different kinds of internships. By seeing that you've done them, along with a portfolio of your work, we have a much better sense of what your capabilities are."

Advertising sales positions are not necessarily located in the same offices or even cities as the publishing company. Large magazine companies have established sales offices distributed nationwide, and sometimes even worldwide. For example, under the masthead in *Better Homes and Gardens*, you will find sales departments located in Des Moines, Iowa, as well as in Minneapolis, Atlanta, Dallas, San Francisco, Chicago, and Detroit. Each of these sales divisions is responsible for group and individual sales in their region.

You may not have to travel far from your hometown to find the position you want in magazine marketing and advertising sales. Then again, these departments offer many relocation options. The fields of marketing and advertising offer not only flexibility but also possibility.

Taking It to the Streets: Circulation and Distribution

7

All the hard work involved in creating a magazine is wasted if the magazine does not find its way into the readers' hands. Selling the magazine through subscriptions and retail outlets is another essential component of magazine publishing. The circulation and distribution departments connect the magazine with its readers.

John Chilson, an author and consultant, runs his own company, Circulation Solutions. He has worked in the magazine circulation and distribution field for twenty years. John often tells this story to illustrate the importance of these departments. "A husband and wife wanted to start their own architectural magazine. The man called me to consult. He had this beautiful architectural magazine, printed in full color on expensive paper. He'd sold a lot of advertising space and bought some excellent articles. But now he had 100,000 printed copies sitting in a warehouse and no way to get them to readers. I told him what he had to do to distribute them. I never heard from him again."

As John's story illustrates, producing the finest magazine is meaningless unless you can deliver it to readers. In an advice essay on his Web site (*www.circsolutions.com*), Chilson asks some pointed questions: "Don't publishers, editors, advertising sales people, and production managers realize that, without readers, all the words they write and publish and sell are only the sound of one hand clapping?" Chilson continues, "Not only do these publishers, editors, sales people, and production managers need readers, they need readers who will appreciate, enjoy, use, and desire the words those [people] work so hard to produce."

Unfortunately, such readers are not just hanging around, waiting to fall off a tree. They must be sought after, wooed, and handled with care. "And if you treat them right, you can even get them to pay for the publication," Chilson adds. "But be warned; such readers can be a fickle lot, and without lots of tender loving care, they may quickly disappear."

Selling Subscriptions

It takes a dedicated team to successfully increase subscription numbers. Some magazines rely on well-established techniques. For instance, *Successful Farming* magazine publisher Jim McCormick sells subscriptions using two different methods.

"We have about forty independent field agents who go farm to farm, selling and renewing subscriptions," McCormick says. "We have managers who supervise renewals through the mail as well, because we have readers who prefer not to have a sales person call on them. It's split about fifty-fifty." Additionally, circulation staff members monitor subscription expiration dates and send out renewal notices hoping to retain existing subscribers. Consequently, *Successful Farming* magazine has the largest prepaid subscription readership of any farm magazine in America, with a circulation of more than 465,000. In general, circulation departments are staffed in the following manner:

Circulation Director

Oversees all circulation marketing and subscription fulfillment. She or he conducts budgeting and circulation forecasting.

Circulation Manager

Responsible for the marketing of one or more publications; in a smaller publishing company, he or she may also be responsible for fulfillment, ensuring that subscribers receive their magazine in a timely fashion.

Promotions Manager

Promotes the magazine for the purpose of selling subscriptions. He or she may develop business relationships with newsstands and bookstores.

Newsstand Manager/Coordinator

Works with the national and regional newsstand distributors and wholesalers who sell magazines at their sites.

Fulfillment Manager

Responsible for maintaining a specialized database of the readers and subscribers. He or she prepares the label files for mailing the magazine, as well as the renewal notices and subscription invoices.

Each of these people may require at least one assistant. "No exact career path exists for circulation positions," Chilson says, "but there are some skills a candidate will need to be successful in this field. I don't have a college degree, but I did take college courses."

Chilson believes that, "Any general consumer marketing courses would be helpful. Focus on math up through algebra. Familiarity with spreadsheets is very important. But the main skill is an ability to pay attention to detail. There are many, many tasks to be performed, usually on a tight schedule. While most publishers don't actively offer internships, there are some out there."

In any magazine circulation office, the most important job is data entry. John Chilson warns that almost all circulation jobs pay poorly. According to Chilson, circulation managers frequently start out with little or no training, remain in the same position for several years, receive small annual salary increases, and often decide to look for another job. Still, "a number of circulation managers remain in the same position for ten, fifteen, twenty years or more. Unfortunately, these people often give it all up during or after a conversion to a new circulation system because they have difficulty making all the required adjustments."

But Chilson points out that a few circulation managers climb the corporate ladder, migrating into bigger and better publishing companies. They stay for the same reasons Chilson himself has remained in the magazine circulation business. "Being a circulation manager is one of the most exciting and fun jobs in the company. You need never be bored, and there are opportunities for you to become experienced in different areas."

Chilson contends, "The circulation manager has more freedom to define his or her job and daily activities than almost anyone else in any other industry making the same salary." If you want to talk to your readers, start a readership survey. If you want to market, plan a promotion campaign or write some copy. If you want to play with your PC, analyze your circulation database for promotional responses, readership demographics, and renewal rates.

Once the magazine publisher discovers that a staff member understands some facet of magazine circulation, they can obtain a position in the department. As Chilson notes, "One big factor is the range in size of the various publishers. In some cases, I've found that six months ago the circulation manager was the receptionist. No one else in the company had any idea what the circulation department really did."

Distribution Director

Kyle Chowning, former Web development and distribution director for Vox Publishing in Nashville, Tennessee, started in the business as a customer service representative. "I actually had a friend who worked with Vox," Chowning explains. "I have a degree in business management, but I didn't seek out a magazine publisher for my first job. Over the course of three years, I was promoted twice, just recently to the Web development and distribution director's position."

Distributing magazines to retail outlets is an essential component of magazine publishing.

Vox is unique in that it publishes several magazines for the Christian music market with a staff of fifteen. It's a relatively new company. "We work very hard, and many days what we do most is crisis management," Chowning relates. "The downfall of working in a small publishing firm is our work is so diversified we don't have the time or resources to grow as quickly as we'd like."

Chowning believes that another downfall of working with a small publisher is the lack of time to work on larger, long-term projects such as test marketing and direct mail promotions. Chowning characterizes his workplace as one in constant crisis. "I might have a project I'm working on, but I can't spend my entire day focused on it because there are so many other things that need doing," Chowning admits. "As Web manager, I update the company's Web site to reflect each new issue. I'm committed to customer service and spend a lot of time returning telephone calls."

Echoing Chilson, Chowning believes that a good circulation manager pays close attention to detail and has a strong sense of organization. "But," he adds, "success goes beyond those two essential skills. You'll need organization and vision. Those two don't always go together, because an orderly thinker doesn't usually have the flights of fancy, the imagination, of a person with vision. This position takes a person who can improvise, who can develop an organizational matrix. No school can prepare a person for this work."

One way distribution and circulation managers improve their techniques is through networking and professional organizations. "Going to luncheons with colleagues in the business helps me find contacts to share ideas and facilitate my work, especially on the Internet," Chowning notes. "We have one disadvantage in that Vox is a fairly exclusive market. But we can still use some of the same resources and ideas."

Despite the drawbacks, he finds his work quite rewarding. "It can be a lot of fun. You'll find yourself building a circulation and distribution program through trial and error until you develop a control package of your most successful efforts. Then you can try new promotions and sales plans based on that control package."

After nearly three years as Web manager and distribution director for Vox, Chowning is planning to freelance as a Web site designer at home. In today's economy, moving frequently from job to job is not uncommon. Nationwide studies have indicated that the average adult will migrate through seven different jobs in a lifetime.

The skills Chowning developed during his time at Vox should prove helpful in his new business. He has sharpened a number of skills that he can apply to many other kinds of work. Plus, he has built a valuable network of contacts.

A Growing Field

"Circulation isn't rocket science—it's a numbers game," Chilson points out. "But right now I've seen more jobs posted for circulation managers and staff than I've seen in twenty years in the field. Back in the early 1990s, magazines had some financial difficulties and downsized many of their departments. Now they are finding the need to rebuild those departments. I feel the job market for circulation positions will hold strong for at least another couple of years."

Marketing the increasing number of Internet e-zines (magazines published solely on-line) is another swiftly growing professional field. "Web skills are going to become key to circulation success," he argues. "One company I work with normally sends out between 400,000 and 500,000 direct-mail subscription and renewal pieces annually. When they switched to DEM— direct e-mail—it saved them a lot of money in printing and postage, plus the pay-up rate doubled."

This is a groundbreaking area of the circulation process that will continue to grow. "Within strict guidelines, publishers can promote hard-copy magazines on the Internet, or they can publish the magazine itself as an e-zine online. This last method saves millions of dollars in paper, printing, and postage," Chilson observes.

E-zines have the potential to reach countless readers. As laptop and hand-held computer technology advances and the cost of these convenient, portable tools decreases, e-zines will reach more and more readers. With these advances, circulation and distribution departments are on the move.

Many people often overlook the twin fields of circulation and distribution when considering a career in magazine publishing. But you might find this work enjoyable. Furthermore, a position in circulation or distribution can serve as a stepping stone to other magazine careers.

Finding the Right Fit

In addition to choosing a particular career, there are other questions to consider in your job search: Which size publishing company is your best bet? Would you prefer working in a major city, a smaller community, or at home? Happily, magazine publishing companies come in all shapes and sizes.

Large Publishing Houses

If you decide to work for a larger magazine, your job will more than likely focus on a single aspect of the magazine's creation and distribution. For example, if you work for *Newsweek* or *People*, you will be one of hundreds of people in a single department. Not surprisingly, the majority of these publishing houses are located in the world's largest cities such as New York, Los Angeles, Chicago, San Francisco, London, Paris, Rome, and Berlin. One advantage of working for a larger company is that opportunities for advancement are usually proportionate to the size of the company.

Medium Publishing Houses

In many ways, medium-sized publishing houses resemble large houses. Both require you to meet deadlines, pay close attention to detail, and work well on your own and with others. However, medium-sized houses can offer more job flexibility. Robert Silvers, executive publisher of *The Saturday Evening Post* for twenty-nine years, discusses his career path and working environment. "We have five separate departments of the type you'd traditionally find in a publishing office: editorial, art, advertising and sales, production, and circulation. Together, as a staff of seventy, we publish the *Post* bi-monthly, as well as seven children's magazines." While staff members have specific duties, Silvers says they all work together on every aspect of the publishing process, much like an extended family or community.

"It's an informally structured environment," Silvers adds. "We work hard to maintain the familiar *Saturday Evening Post* format that families once received weekly (now every two months), with the Norman Rockwell covers, the kinds of features they love, and all their favorite cartoons drawn from our archives." Now owned and operated by a nonprofit organization, *The Saturday Evening Post* was, at one time, an immensely popular general interest consumer magazine published by the Curtis Publishing Company. At the height of its popularity, the *Post* had a circulation of 6 million.

"In February 1969, Curtis decided to shut down publication of the *Post*," Silvers explains. "General interest magazines were losing popularity and it's harder to sell space in them than it is in magazines with a more narrow focus. The Children's Better Health Institute wanted

McGraw-Hill in New York City is a large magazine publisher.

to buy the rights to *Jack and Jill* magazine from Curtis. In the process, the Institute ended up with all of the magazine rights."

Not all general interest magazines find it difficult to sell advertising space. Currently, *Reader's Digest* has a circulation of more than 18 million. "If a magazine has what we call 'vitality,' meaning it's viable and growing, then being general interest isn't a problem," remarks Silvers. "It's easy to sell the magazine if you have everything lined up and going for you."

The Children's Better Health Institute hired Silvers in 1971 when it resumed publication of *The Saturday Evening Post* on a bi-monthly basis. He has been the executive publisher ever since. While about 40 percent of the magazine's current editorial material now centers on health-related issues, the staff has worked to maintain the charm that made *The Saturday Evening Post* one of America's most popular general interest magazines.

"The *Post* now has a circulation of 400,000, and is mailed primarily to subscribers. We don't sell many copies on the newsstands because the dealers prefer to stock magazines that are published more frequently, thus pulling buyers back more often. The seven children's magazines have a combined circulation of 1.2 million," says Silvers. "While I spend most of my time on duties connected to the sales and marketing of these magazines, I also do some nontraditional things as well."

Silvers says he organizes the "Tulip Time Scholarship Games" each April, in which hundreds of young students are invited to compete for college scholarships. "I just spent most of the past month calling colleges and asking for scholarships. That's one thing that's really nice about working in a larger publishing house for a magazine with strong name recognition. I'm able to call just about anyone and say, 'I'm calling from *The Saturday Evening Post*,' and they know right away who we are. It's a good feeling."

Small Publishing Houses

Depending on where you live, or want to live, you may find working for a relatively small publisher quite rewarding. The size of its staff typically reflects the size of its budget. Each person performs many tasks at these small, often literary, magazines. Consequently, you can gain a broad and varied understanding of the ins and outs of magazine publishing.

Short Stuff for Grown-Ups is a literary magazine published in Loveland, Colorado. Editor Donna Bowman works with a full-time copy editor and art director. The magazine is designed and composed in-house. In order to save money, Bowman sub-contracts magazine production and distribution (printing and mailing).

"I've worked for more than thirty years as an editor, mainly in newspapers but also in broadcasting," says Bowman. "In that capacity, I realized that for a creative writer, the toughest part was getting published in the first place. That's why I started *Short Stuff* and why I keep it open to all freelancers, whether or not they've been published before."

Multi-magazine publishers such as Meredith Corporation, Hearst Corporation, or Rodale offer positions in large-circulation magazines as well as smaller ones. If you find a job with Meredith, for example, you might be working on the staff of *Ladies Home Journal* or *Successful Farming*. Deciding what size publishing house or where you want to work is not something you are likely to do right now. It will take some soul-searching, career exploration, hands-on experience, and possibly two to four years of college or vocational school before you have a true feel for where you want to fit into this constantly changing career field.

What You Need to Do Now

In previous chapters, you learned from experienced professionals what to do to prepare for various careers in this field. While some employers are willing to train a new recruit for a specific position, there are skills you should acquire before applying. David Johnson, a guidance and careers counselor for Hononegah High School in Rockton, Illinois, offers suggestions as to how you might position yourself for a career in media, including magazine publishing.

"High school is more than the final four years of traditional education," Johnson explains. "It's a transition in more ways than one, a transition from child to adult that more or less occurs in a familiar pattern." Johnson observes, "When students enter high school as freshmen there's a lot happening in their lives emotionally. Changing from middle school to high school is somewhat like dropping off a fifty-story building. As counselors, we're aware of this reaction, and are prepared to make it less traumatic."

One Teacher's Advice

Hononegah High School journalism teacher David Sennerud says that, "Right now, the big career choice is in broadcasting." Sennerud adds, "Some of my students have mentioned working in print or newspapers, and a couple have talked about some phase of magazine work. But no matter which field they choose, they'll need to know how to write well."

Sennerud feels that the evolution of computerized publishing programs and software such as PageMaker has changed writing styles. For example, formerly when writing a newspaper assignment, writers composed feature stories "pyramid style." Because reporters never knew what the editor might cut, they ordered facts according to their importance to the story. Now, with digitized measuring, writers need not order the information in their stories in that way.

Sennerud often discusses career options in magazine publishing with his students. "We discuss magazine career opportunities along with the other choices," Sennerud says. "Primarily, we've talked about freelance writing, especially for the trade magazines. The trades are as slick and impressive as consumer magazines. They are well written and well read, even by those not in the field. That's because trade publishers and editors work hard to give their magazines a good look and reader appeal."

Sennerud believes that trade magazines are a great place to start as an entry-level writer or editorial assistant. Even if a student also chooses to work in broadcast journalism, he or she can write freelance for magazines at the same time. The two careers complement each other. "One of the projects we do in class is to analyze a magazine. We break it down to see how much editorial is involved, how many pages are devoted to briefs, and letters to the editor, and how the advertising is distributed. We also analyze the best features drawn from current issues of magazines such as *Rolling Stone*."

One thing Sennerud has noticed is that creative people tend to be "jacks of all trades." They might work at a local newspaper writing sports or features. Additionally, they may be involved in their high school's newspaper and yearbook. "They may not necessarily be considering a major in English or journalism, but they're active in those areas for love of the work." He adds, "When we see this happening, we encourage these students to pursue their skills, either as a career or on a freelance basis. We want them to stay involved." Regardless of career path, Sennerud stresses that writing, desktop publishing, and graphic arts skills are essential in today's Internet-connected world.

T-Zines

One way to explore writing is to become familiar with emerging t-zines, magazines written by teenagers for teenagers. "Magazine publishers are catering to teens more today than ever before," Sennerud adds. "Hononegah regularly receives letters from these publishers asking for submissions from our journalism students. High-school level writing and publishing is

Students and a teacher discuss magazine publishing.

becoming nationally recognized as having a valid audience, and these publishers need writers." Indeed, these publishers and editors are so committed to launching high school student writing careers that they regularly attend national journalism conventions looking for unpublished young writers. "I always make my students aware of these opportunities," says Sennerud.

Analyze Magazines

Gather the magazines in your home that interest you, or visit your school or public library and explore the magazine stacks. Begin by reading the masthead, where you can count the number of editors, writers, photographers, graphic artists, production heads, advertising directors, and assistants the magazine employs as well as their areas of responsibility.

Study the table of contents for the issue. Scan through the features and regular columns, and gather a feel for the magazine's readership. After comparing two or three issues of a magazine, you will begin to understand more about its format and focus. You will also learn how many photographs the magazine uses regularly, and the amount of artwork developed to accompany the features, columns, and briefs.

Examine advertising space. Check out which companies place ads and how their products relate to readers' interests and needs. Does the publisher place advertising on a feature's opening page, or does the advertising surround the copy that continues on the following pages? What percentage of the staff is devoted to selling advertising space? How many regional advertising offices are listed in the masthead? Where are they located?

How did the magazine arrive at its final destination? You or your parents may subscribe to this magazine. Maybe you buy a copy at the store whenever you see an article that interests you listed on the cover. Perhaps your school or public library receives copies of the magazine because it is popular with students or library users. Exploring these questions will help you gain a more complete sense of the publishing process.

Create Your Own Magazine

After you have a solid understanding of magazine construction, try designing and composing your own magazine. Begin by determining a subject or focus, for example, photography. Perhaps, name your magazine using a short, clever phrase related to photography. Decide on the length of your magazine and the size of the paper you will use.

Next, work on the table of contents. You need to determine how many feature articles you want to publish, and whether you want to write an editorial column about some aspect of photography. Design the features pages by balancing the copy with strong, compelling photographs.

As this is a photography magazine, you might solicit ads from local camera stores, film processors, book sellers, and other related businesses. Decide where to place the advertisements. Sketch in their ads based on what you learned by evaluating other magazines.

Once the magazine itself is designed, develop a plan for distribution and subscriptions fulfillment. Putting together a new magazine single-handedly is hard work, but by doing so, you gain an elementary understanding of magazine publishing. In turn, you can decide whether to explore magazine publishing further.

Magazines of the Future: E-Newsletters and E-Zines

If you have ever dreamed of publishing your own magazine, the time is ripe. The development of the Internet has eliminated the most costly aspects of publishing, printing, and distribution. You can create your own on-line magazine or newsletter. You can help build cyber communities. The possibilities are endless!

Michael Gorman produces his own Web site, The Scum Worm (*http://members.aol.com/nycgorman/home.html*). He discusses discovering the power of on-line publishing in an essay on his site. "When I was about ten, I published a fun little newsletter, my own version of *MAD*," Gorman recalls. "I passed it around to my friends, who laughed and giggled at my wit. The problem was that they had to give it back to me once they were done reading it, because it was the only copy I had."

Gorman explains that, at the time, his only copying resource was a mimeograph machine. Although he had already written, edited, and composed the newsletter on a typewriter, there was no practical way for him to reproduce or distribute it. "A few years later in eighth grade, I started drawing up these mini-comics based on a superhero named Super Kool Kat." Gorman continues, "Our library had regular copy machines, but the problem was I didn't have the money to pay for printing copies of my comics. Once again, I had to pass the original copies around from friend to friend."

Gorman stopped creating comics fairly quickly, as his financial situation did not improve. "My attitude was why bother spending the time drawing up this whole comic that I couldn't afford to have printed?" Gorman adds, "Luckily, in college, I had a friend working at a major book publisher who could get my printing done for free on the office copy machine. Getting free copying is quite an amazing thing, especially for a broke art student."

Gorman began publishing his comics again, giving out copies to all his friends. "I even began charging money for my comics," he notes. "This was a cool thing. I continue to put out comics to this day, but of course, not being a kid any more, I have the money to pay for my own printing."

In 1995, just as Gorman published his comic, *Air Guitar*, a friend told him about the "zine world." "Before then, I thought I was, like, the only guy self-publishing comics anymore, carrying the torch for R. Crumb and all those '60s underground artists," Gorman admits. "Boy, I couldn't have been more wrong."

Gorman explains that he discovered thousands of people worldwide doing the same thing. "I was both shocked and furious that I didn't know about this sooner. There seems to be a publication for every interest you can think of, and a publication for things you'd never believe would be in print. And all these glorious publications are produced by regular Joes, like you and me. Then the Web hit. The Web hit hard."

Now anyone can easily access the Web, produce HTML documents to post on the Web, and say whatever they want. "Imagine me at ten years old being able to produce that newsletter as an HTML document, posting it on the Web, registering it to a bunch of search engines, and getting actual responses from around the globe via e-mail," Gorman muses. "Think about not even having to worry about printing or distribution costs. The world could have seen and commented on the saga of Super Kool Kat, not just a group of my friends."

While Gorman self-started his career as an on-line publisher, others have worked their way into this new field through more conventional channels. Kate Schultz operates two informative Web sites about Internet publishing: *www.e-zinez.com* and *www.ezineuniversity.com*. Schultz holds a master's in business administration and has worked a variety of jobs: computer programmer, manager, systems administrator, technical writer, and trainer.

"Before I started my career as a programmer, I worked as a temp doing clerical, secretarial, word processing, and desktop publishing for several years," says Schultz. "This experience, more than anything, let me look at how different industries all share some of the same challenges." Schultz's programming and management experience taught her how important communication is with end users during a programming life cycle. This knowledge led to conducting user group meetings, training seminars, and publishing newsletters for her company's computer users.

"There are many routes to publishing. I took the long one," Schultz recalls. "I started my *e-zinez.com* site after creating sites for some of my clients. Start-up wasn't difficult because it was an add-on to my consulting business for Web development and programming."

Schultz has sound advice to share with those who want to get started on their own e-zine. "For those just starting out, make sure you are properly funded to start up or, in other words, don't quit your day job until you are successful with your publishing venture." You need to find a publishing topic or subject that you are passionate about, whether it is music, fashion, computers, sports, cooking and food, or gardening. Finding a niche in the e-zine market will give your publication a strong focus and draw like-minded readers to your site. "If you love what you do, then it doesn't seem like work," Schultz adds. "If you retain your enthusiasm, interest, and passion for your topic, it will be visible to your readers. Of course, having a passion for what you do also makes it much easier for those twelve-hour workdays!"

Management and organizational skills are critical to success. "Skills and education really depend upon which part of the publishing field you want to enter," Schultz advises. "If you want to run an on-line publishing company, a business background will help the most." And, Schultz warns, "It's not uncommon for new start-up on-line publishers to perform all of those job functions, including Webmaster."

Sound interesting? But how does an e-zine publisher make money? Schultz explains, "One way most on-line publishers make money is the same way traditional ones make money, via advertising revenue or as a venue to sell your own products or services." She continues, "The big difference between e-zine and hard copy magazines is that most on-line publishers don't

Organizational skills, as well as the ability to work well with others, are essential to e-zine publishing.

charge for subscriptions. Because of this, e-zine publishers miss out on one of the huge revenue generators of traditional publishing."

As you may recall from a previous chapter, John Chilson has a consulting business called Circulation Solutions. He also has his own Web site with e-zine-style articles and tips at *www.circsolutions.com*, which you can access and read. Along with a lot of free advice, Chilson is advertising his consulting services and the books he has written about subscription and circulation functions of the magazine publishing business. This is how Chilson makes money from his Web site. "You really need to have advertisers lined up or a product or service of your own to sell before you start publishing," Schultz advises. "Another option is to sign up for affiliate programs and sell products for other companies, so you can receive commissions on those sales. *Amazon.com* probably has the best-known affiliate program on the Internet."

Getting Started

To start your own e-zine, there are many things that experts say you will need to know and do. Obviously, you need strong computer skills. In fact, there is a good chance you will become your own Webmaster and administrator. You should start to learn as much as you can about how the Internet operates, as well as how to establish Web sites, register with search engines, and design on-line. You will want to become familiar with Adobe PageMaker, PhotoShop, and related software programs.

Find your niche. General interest e-zines can get lost on-line, while those that focus narrowly on a subject have a built-in pool of potential readers. Are you passionate about woodworking? Beanie Babies? Stitchery? Cooking and developing new recipes? Camping? Off-road biking? Choose a topic or product that you know your friends are interested in as well and you will have a built-in audience.

Do the marketing and research necessary to evaluate how well your new e-zine will be received. Start by visiting all the related e-zines and analyzing their sites. Can you offer more? Something totally different? Can you write and edit features and tips that go above and beyond what your competitors are publishing? Can you update them on a monthly basis? Is the market for your topic saturated; are there already too many e-zines dedicated to this subject?

Ask yourself what you want to achieve as far as income is concerned. Are you going to publish this e-zine just for the pleasure of sharing your expertise? Perhaps this will become a second source of income; a freelance project in addition to your full-time career. Or is an e-zine something you believe will generate enough income that you can operate it full time?

If you want to make money in this on-line venture, how are you going to do it? You will need to develop unique products, patterns, or services to sell. In addition, you might find advertisers to help underwrite the costs of publishing an e-zine. Now search for potential affiliates or companies that make products or provide services that are compatible with your topic. Linking your e-zine with their Web sites can pay off in commissions.

No matter how far you carry this exercise, you will gain some understanding of the nature of e-zines. Publishing an e-zine sounds like fun but, as Schultz points out, it is also a lot of hard work. As in every other sort of business or industry, there is an element of risk. Not every e-zine succeeds.

Experts strongly recommend that you build a strong foundation of knowledge based on education and experience. Schultz and Gorman worked in related fields for several years before they launched their respective on-line careers. You might consider starting a Web page dedicated to happenings around your school or community with a group of like-minded friends. You could also talk to career counselors and advisers about forming an e-zine club at school in which you explore on-line publishing with the help of computer science and journalism teachers. Regardless of how you approach the exciting prospect of online publishing, anything you do now toward learning more about this field will prove useful down the road.

Glossary

clips Copies of published articles, photographs, artwork, and finished advertising pieces which can be included with résumés, submitted manuscripts, and job applications to demonstrate a person's experience and abilities.

composition The act of putting together an entire magazine by combining its separate parts; originally the work or skill of setting type.

demographics From demography, the statistical science of population distribution; in publishing, the term describes the segment of the population considered to be potential readers.

dummy A preliminary set of pages with editorial and advertising materials roughly sketched in, from which a finished magazine issue is developed.

e-zines Magazines which are published on the Internet; they may be available exclusively on the Internet, or may be partial or total reproductions of the traditional hard copy issues.

freelance Any writer, editor, photographer, or artist who is not under contract with, nor employed by, a publisher and who sells his or her work or services to more than one client at a time.

graphics Design, including the use of type, employed in visual representation; in magazines, the sum of all its visual parts including type, photography, and art.

keyline The process of pasting down art and photography and setting type on a board or heavy paper to produce a page; also, the finished product.

layout The manner in which a magazine is arranged; the plan or make-up of the magazine. Also, the actual page or magazine. Layout can be used as a verb or noun.

masthead The box or section printed in every magazine issue listing the publisher, owners, editors, staff writers, and artists, as well as the location of the magazine's offices, subscription rates, and more.

portfolio A selection of representative works by a writer, artist, photographer, graphics expert, or editor.

query letter A letter sent by writers, artists, and photographers to prospective publishers asking if they would be interested in considering a finished piece.

typography The art and process of setting type for printing, as well as the arrangement, style, and general appearance of materials printed from type.

'zines The shortened name given to alternative magazines produced by underground artists and writers on a wide range of subjects.

For More Information

In the United States

American Institute of Graphic Arts
164 Fifth Avenue
New York, NY 10010
(212) 255-4004
e-mail: info@aiga.org
Web site: http://www.aiga.org

American Society of Magazine Editors
919 Third Avenue, 22nd Floor
New York, NY 10022
(212) 872-3700
e-mail: asme@magazine.org
Web site: http://asme.magazine.org

In Canada

Periodical Writers Association of Canada
54 Wolseley Street, Suite 203
Toronto, ON M5T 1A5
(416) 504-1645
e-mail: pwac@web.net
Web site: http://www.pwac.ca

Web Sites

Chip Rowe's *The Book of Zines*
http://www.zinebook.com

Editor & Publisher On-Line
http://www.mediainfo.com

JournalismJobs.com
http://www.journalismjobs.com

Publish Media
http://www.publish.com

PubList.com, the Internet Directory of Publications
http://www.publist.com

The Quill Society
http://www.quill.net/home/index.htm

Writer's Digest
http://www.writersdigest.com

For Further Reading

Bly, Robert W. *Business-to-Business Direct Marketing: Proven Direct Response Methods to Generate More Leads and Sales*. Lincolnwood, IL: NTC Business Books, 1998.

_____*The Copywriter's Handbook: A Step-By-Step Guide to Writing Copy That Sells*. New York: Henry Holt, 1990.

Chilson, John M. *Circulation for Fun and Profit*. Hightstown, NJ: Primedia Intertec, 1999.

Eberts, Marjorie, and Rachel Kelsey. *Careers for Cybersurfers & Other Online Types*. Lincolnwood, IL: VGM Career Horizons, 1997.

Holm, Kirsten C., and Donya Dickerson (eds.). *2000 Writer's Market*. Cincinnati, OH: Writer's Digest Books, 2000.

Mackay, Harvey. *Beware the Naked Man Who Offers You His Shirt*. New York: Ballantine Books, 1996.

Pirillo, Chris. *Poor Richard's E-mail Publishing*. Lakewood, CO: Top Floor Publishing, 1999.

Index

Credits

Photo Credits

Cover photo by © AFP/Corbis; p .2 © Christel Gerstenberg/Corbis; p. 6 © AFP/Corbis; p. 10 © Superstock; p. 17 © Telegraph Colour Library/FPG; p. 23 © Michael Malyszko/FPG; p. 28 © Gary Buss/FPG; p. 34 © Ron Chapple/FPG; p. 37 © Robert Maass/Corbis; p. 41 © Photomondo/FPG; pp. 46 and 88 © Corbis; p. 49 © Paul Souders/Corbis; p. 52 © James Marshall/Corbis; p. 58 © Stephen Simpson/FPG; p. 62 © VCG/FPG; p. 67 © R.W. Jones/Corbis; p. 77 © Paul Almasy/Corbis; p. 83 © Vince Streano/Corbis; p. 95 © Superstock.

Series Design
Danielle Goldblatt

Layout
Les Kanturek